e-Commerce Taxes
Tax Planning for the Online Retailer

By: Jason Taylor

See us online at: cyberspacecpa.com

info@cyberspacecpa.com

ISBN: 978-0-9920569-3

D1292361

Table of Contents

Introduction and Professional Disclosure:

I have been working with online clients for several years now. Every tax season I find new clients that have been paying way too much in taxes. This isn't right. And the problem comes down to one item: knowledge is power as the saying goes.

My goal for this book is to help spread knowledge. I come from a family of entrepreneurs and small business owners. We are in business to make money, not pay taxes. I imagine you have the same objective. The government recognizes this as well. Small businesses make up more than 50% of the gross domestic production (GDP). Small businesses provide jobs, circulate money, and increase local economies. With this understanding, congress has passed several laws to provide tax relief to business owners, what the lay person would call loopholes. I like to call these loopholes what they actual are: incentives for people to start businesses.

All too often, people start businesses without knowledge of the tax laws that they can take advantage of. Without the proper elections and understanding of the laws you can end up paying more than 50% of your profits in taxes. No one wants to lose half of their income to taxes. The government doesn't even want anyone to pay that much in taxes. Regular wages earners pay more taxes than any other group and they don't even pay 50% in taxes.

As a business owner, the government wants you to hire wage earners. It is ridiculous to think that you should be paying higher taxes than the people you employ. You are carrying all the risk of ownership and should be compensated for that risk. If there was more incentive to be a regular wage earner then there wouldn't be any small businesses. The reality is that congress understand this and expects you to pay less taxes than your employees (as percentage of income), not more.

In this book, I hope to very clearly illustrate how the tax code can be your friend instead of your enemy. Everyone hates taxes. Usually, this is because you pay so much in taxes. But taxes are a requirement of society that we will never get rid of. So, let's make sure we are staying compliant to keep the tax man off our backs but also taking full advantage of the incentives that congress has given to start and run a business. Otherwise you are better off just going to get a 9-5 job at a factory and earn your salary.

As with all books written by a professional we are required to make a disclosure that in no way is this book intended as tax advice or should be used for preparing your own taxes. It is intended as information to help you have a better conversation with your tax professional. The examples are provided as illustration only and are a close approximation to the actual tax rates and formulas. Please consult with a professional before applying any of the suggestions given in this book.

This book was written prior to the passage of the 2018 Tax Reform Bill. After careful study of the new bill I have decided to not make any changes to this book. This book is primarily concerned with the calculation of income. The 2018 Tax Reform Bill primarily changes the tax treatment after income has been calculated. The only changes required in this book to be in full compliance with the 2018 Tax Reform Bill would be the changing the tax rates after taxable net income has been determined, to remove the personal exemption amount, increase the standard deduction, and include the 20% tax break for investment income from passthrough entities.

The personal exemption and standard deduction would make an unnoticeable change in calculating the tax due. The brackets used in the calculation of the tax due and including the 20% tax break for investment income would make a significant difference in the amount of tax due. However, the changes would be favorable and would only illustrate the point of the book stronger by decreasing the tax due by switching from a Sch C to a passthrough entity.

Chapter 1: Please Meet our Fictional Business Sunny Day Sports

Throughout this book I will be using a company called Sunny Day Sports. The owner of this company is Frank. He is married and has two young children living at home. Sunny Day Sports is an online retail store selling through Amazon FBA, his own website using Shopify, Walmart, eBay, and other ecommerce marketplaces. You can refer to the Appendix for illustrations of the tax that Frank is required to pay under the various strategies that will be discussed throughout this book.

Prior to contacting a CPA, Sunny Day Sports had sales of $200,000. After the cost of the inventory Frank purchased and a few other business expenses, Frank figured he had a net profit of $100,000. Easy numbers for easy math. However, the more I have worked with online retailers, these numbers are about average for someone that has been selling for a couple of years online and has built their brand through good advertising.

Frank started Sunny Day Sports all on his own. He had read a few blogs and did some research about how to build his brand and set up his store with Amazon. He had his website built by a designer and got everything set up through Shopify. After a couple of years, he was very happy with his growth and found that the online retail was providing enough work that he could no longer keep his day job. He quit and went to work full time on Sunny Day Sports.

However, when he went to do his taxes he quickly discovered that all the quick growth also resulted in some high taxes. This is cash that he just doesn't have as he needs to purchase additional inventory to sell, pay his bills and put food on the table. Not to mention he has enjoyed spending a little more time with his family and was thinking about taking his wife to dinner and a movie. But after the tax software showed him the $28,700 tax bill he owed. He didn't know what to do.

Unfortunately, this is an all too common problem. But the best part about stories is that we can change them. After filing his taxes in April last year, instead of just continuing with the status quo, he heard about some tax strategies and called a CPA for advice. Frank shopped around for the right CPA. He found one that understood his business, e-commerce. Frank had originally avoided CPAs thinking they were too expensive for what they provided. But after shopping around, he found one that promised to cost less than the savings the CPA would provide.

Instead of going the entire year doing the same as the year before, the CPA and Frank worked together to ensure Frank's tax bill was going to be less, even with growth. The CPA said it all started with a formal registration of his business with the Secretary of State.

Chapter 2: Formation of the Business

The first step in lowering taxes is to have your business set up right. A limited liability company, AKA LLC, is a legal structure for businesses that provide countless benefits to owners.

The number one benefit of an LLC is outside the scope of this book and my expertise. LLC starts with the word limited because this business structure provides limited risk to the owners. Risk has all sorts of meanings so to simplify let's just say risk = chance of a law suit.

In online retail, we should be worried about the products we are selling and how they could affect our customers, *social responsibility*. Using our example company, Frank picked up a pallet of sunscreen at a discount that was overstock at a department store. He posts it in his Amazon store. No big deal right. Hopefully, that is right and nine times out of ten it will be as most items are ran through many tests before beginning sent to market. But what if (*yes, there are a thousand what ifs*) it turns out that this batch of sunscreen got past quality and control with a bad ingredient in it and several of the customers who purchased the sunscreen from Sunny Day Sports end up in the hospital with rashes. The doctors confirm it is from the sunscreen and the health insurance companies file a law suit. The insurance companies sue everyone in the sales chain: manufacturer, distributor, and retailer (Frank).

In a situation like this, as the online retailer, you don't have the deepest pockets, nor are you most culpable so you aren't going to carry the brunt of the law suit. **However, you could be the most vulnerable if you don't have an LLC**. If the insurance companies win, the judge could find you 10% at fault and without an LLC to protect you, your car and home could go on the chopping block to pay for your portion of the damages awarded. While those really at fault, the manufacturer, will get a much higher percentage of fault. But the employees, officers, and shareholders at the manufacturer all have their personal property protected behind the corporate veil.

In this example, you have big brother manufacturer to help in the law suit as they will be considered most liable. They will pay for the attorney to fight the case. But let's change the story a little bit. Your manufacturer is in China and out of reach of the US court system or you purchased the product from a local person that is advertising homemade, organic sunscreen. Now you have the deepest pockets. You get the picture. This is an example of *risk = chance of a law suit* and how damaging it could be to you.

Does this stop us from doing business? **NO!** We are entrepreneurs and live with this type of risk every day. But we can limit our risk by getting our personal assets protected behind that same corporate veil that the manufacturing company provided to their shareholders. And if a law suit does come, your attorney will be able to defend you better and make sure you keep your home if you have LLC.

The secondary benefit of the LLC is where the scope of this book lies. The LLC provides several options to business owners for tax planning. The best tax planning starts right here. Without the LLC, any tax savings strategies are severely limited.

The LLC provides freedom in electing how the IRS will tax the business. Federal tax law does not recognize the LLC business structure. The state governments issue LLC designations. Because the IRS does not recognize the LLC, you are able to elect to have your business taxed by any one of the recognized methods.

There are four primary types of tax structures for a business, these are made up of the following:

A *single member LLC* defaults to Schedule C on your individual tax return. This form is called a *disregarded entity* and is the worst option to use when trying to save on taxes. Avoid a Schedule C business unless your CPA strictly suggests using it. Usually that suggestion is only the case if your business is not making enough profit to warrant the cost of going to a higher level.

A *multiple member LLC* defaults to a *partnership*. Better than a Schedule C as it provides a few additional benefits but, still unable to take the largest tax savings strategies available. Same as with the disregarded entity, a partnership should only be used if your CPA suggests using it. Many times, a partnership is used because of the relationship between owners. *LLCs that are owned by a married couple defaults to a partnership and there are only a very few reasons that a married couple should stay a partnership.* If you and your spouse are members in your LLC and you are being taxed as a partnership strongly consider the following paragraphs about corporations.

The next two levels available to an LLC are made through filing elections with the IRS. The first is a *corporation* the second is a *subchapter S corporation* or *S-Corp* for short. Of the two, the S-Corp is the sweet spot for tax savings. However, there are some restrictions. The biggest restriction is that all the owners must be

US citizens. In online retail, I have found that many businesses have foreign partners that are helping to secure inventory. At this point you should decide which is a better option, paying self-employment tax if you elect to be treated as a partnership or paying the double taxation that plagues corporations. This is a more in-depth topic than the scope of this book. If you do fall into this this category, you need to have a good conversation on tax planning with your CPA. You could also consider treating the foreign partner as a subcontractor instead.

In most cases, it is better to avoid a corporation as everything gets locked in the corporation unless you want to pay dividend taxes. Tax planning is much harder for corporations. There are still planning opportunities for tax savings but there is much more freedom in a S-Corp.

The number one best option for online retail is to elect to be taxed as an *S-Corporation*. As a S-Corp you get the best of a corporation without a lot of the drawbacks. S-Corps also benefit from a lot of the freedoms that a disregarded entity (Sch. C) has.

The S-Corp does not suffer from double taxation. Net income (*revenue minus expenses*) is taxed at the individual level. Once the net income is taxed you can withdraw funds from the business without suffering from dividend tax. This is the same freedom that disregarded entities or partnerships offer. You can remove cash from the business and you will not have to pay additional taxes.

The problem with disregarded entities and partnerships is that the owners cannot be employees. Instead, the IRS considered all the net income (revenue minus expenses, or percentage of net income in a partnership) as their wages. This is where the self-employment taxes come from.

Every employed person working for wages or considered self-employed must pay Medicare and Social Security tax. The two types of taxes combined is **15.3%** of your active income (wages). Regular employees split the cost with their employers. They have 7.65% withheld from their pay checks and the other 7.65% is an expense for the business, lowering the business' net (taxable) income.

When a person earns wages, or is actively participating in the management of their company, it is called *active income* and is always subject to Medicare and Social Security tax. When a person does not actively participate in the management it is called *passive income*. This is because they make money without having to do any work. Passive investors get paid back for investing in the business. Passive income derives from investment type activities and is not subject to Medicare or Social Security tax.

In our example business of Sunny Day Sports, Frank is definingly an active participant. His spouse we could argue either way but will treat her as passive so we don't have to pay the Medicare and Social Security tax for her. The two young children are passive now but we will make them active later in this book and discuss why.

Corporations are the only entities that allow a shareholder to also be an employee, both active (*employee*) and passive (*shareholder*). S-Corps also get this benefit. By treating the owners as employees, we can limit the amount of income that is subjected to the 15.3% tax by paying the owners a wage from the corporation. These wages are a business expense which lowers net (*taxable*) income. The remaining net profit is still subject to income tax and since all net income is passed to the owners' individual tax return it combines with the wages you paid yourself and brings you back to the same taxable income you would have had without paying yourself a wage. But, this limited the *active income* which is subject to Medicare and Social Security tax while the remaining income is treated more like *passive income*.

Let's go back to Sunny Day Sports to better understand this principle.

Since Frank has $100,000 of net profit, if he were to file as a partnership (best option without a S-Corp), Frank would receive $50,000 of the net profit which is active income while his wife would get $50,000 as passive income. Because Frank is active, he will have to pay approximately $7,650 of self-employment tax. But if he elects to be taxed as an S-Corp he can limit his active income and pay himself wages of $20,000, cutting his self-employment tax to $3,060. That is an instant $4,590 tax savings.

But Frank wasn't even an LLC to begin with and was filing this taxes as a Schedule C for self-employed income. He must pay self-employment taxes on $98,000 of that net profit which is $14,994 as shown in the first column of the Appendix. Now, just by registering his business as an LLC and electing S-Corp status, he is able to save $11,934 in taxes. **That's almost enough to by a small car.**

That is a lot of savings and way worth the time to properly register and file the election. But why not lower his wages further to $10,000 or $5,000. This is where the court system has stepped in. The tax code states that wages must be fair and reasonable for the work performed. The best way to measure what is fair is to look up the national or regional average for someone doing a similar job. According to Payscale.com, the national average salary for a manager of a small retail store is $44,000. Frank could pay himself that amount which would increase self-employment tax but

$44,000 isn't reasonable. A small retail store isn't going to pay any of their employees 44% of their income. They would go bankrupted trying to pay wages, rent and utilities.

To address this dilemma, courts have ruled what is reasonable. They state that **20% of taxable income is a fair wage** while 80% should be available for dividends or reinvested by the company to grow. This means Frank should pay 20% of net income as his wages until he grows to net income of $220,000. At that point 20 percent is the national average and the fair rule kicks in. From then on, Frank's wages stay at $44,000 with a small raise every couple of years for cost of living.

Even if you don't have enough cash to make payroll, still consider paying yourself. Then contribute the cash back into the company (a paper transaction). This way you can still claim the reasonable deduction in payroll taxes and not have the IRS questioning if you are really a business (we will discuss in the next chapter). Only if you are in the first couple of years of operations or have had several years of losses should you not pay yourself a salary.

Chapter 3: Businesses Rule, Hobbies Drool

This year has been great for Sunny Day Sports. Frank made net profits of $100,000! But to illustrate this chapter better let's go back in time a couple of years. Frank is still working a day job while starting the online retail store on the side. Sunny Day Sports has been fledgling with year after year of losses as Frank has experimented with several different products which did not catch on and sale. After doing some research Frank found that he could write off obsolete inventory to offset his wages from the day job and save on taxes.

He then gets a letter from the IRS saying they want to examine his Schedule C and have requested several items to look at which include the twelve bank statements for the year, a general ledger, tax adjustments, profit and loss, balance sheet, state registration, and a few other items.

Frank, not knowing what a general ledger is Googles it and finds: "the main accounting record of a company or organization." *Accounting records?* He only uses Amazon and they send him a statement every couple of weeks and make a deposit to his bank account. So, he prints off the statements from Amazon and includes an excel file of all the individual sales.

He has been using his personal bank account and prints off his statements highlighting all the expenses that he took on the Schedule C, some of which he couldn't even remember if he had used as business or not. He has never registered with the state. Who has time for that and why should he pay for a registration when he is struggling to get the business going anyway?

He sends off what he has gathered and after a couple of months and several phone calls where he has had to answer questions he gets a letter from the IRS saying that he owes an additional $1,550 in taxes. The IRS stated that they believe his business, Sunny Day Sports is a hobby. They changed his tax return and claimed that his loss on the Schedule C, that had offset his income from his day job was incorrect.

The problem here is that the laws governing the taxation of hobbies states expenses cannot exceed revenue. A hobby cannot ever have a loss. In addition to not being able to claim a loss, expenses also must be directly associated with earning the revenue. Frank had included his cell phone bill and computer as business expenses. The IRS said that those expenses were not directly related to the hobby and denied them. Then they denied some of the other expenses that he had highlighted because he did not have sufficient evidence to justify the expenses as directly related to the hobby. What was left of his expenses were the purchases of inventory.

The remaining expenses allowed by the IRS brought him to a break even on paper, but do to the way the hobby expenses are reported, he still had to pay some tax on the revenue.

Hobby expenses are reported as miscellaneous itemized deductions which are limited by 2% of *adjusted gross income* (AGI) while the revenue is reported as *other income*. To better understand this dilemma, see the following table.

Frank's AGI was adjusted by the IRS to $100,000. His *hobby* expenses were limited by $2,000 (2% if AGI). He had $5,000 of revenue and originally had reported $10,000 of expenses (net loss of $5,000). The IRS limited those expenses to $5,000 but because of the AGI limitation he could only deduct $3,000 on his tax return (this is assuming he has enough expenses to itemize, if not, the expenses disappear in the standard deduction already taken and the situation would be worse).

Not only did he lose the original $5,000 net loss he had reported, he now had to report $3,000 of additional income for a total $8,000 increase to taxable income. This $8,000 increase results in an additional $1,050 taxes with $53 of interest. Frank can always appeal this decision but then he would hire an attorney to represent him in tax court. That will cost a lot more than $1,103.

Change in Taxes After Audited		
	After Audit	Original Taxes
W-2	$95,000	$95,000
Sch C	(5,000)	(5,000)
Original AGI	90,000	90,000
Add back Original Business Loss	5,000	-
Add Hobby Income	5,000	-
New AGI	100,000	90,000
Increase Itemized Deductions ($5000, limited by 2% of AGI)	(15,500)	(12,500)
Exemptions	(16,200)	(16,200)
Taxable Income	68,300	61,300
Tax Due	$9,321	$8,271
Increase in Tax	1,050	
Interest	53	
Amount Due	**$1,103**	

So how do we prevent a small business from having this happen to them?

It's all about presenting the right picture to the IRS. Businesses can go years claiming loss after loss if they can show profit motive. Many CPAs and tax professionals will suggest that three years is the maximum that a business should go with claiming losses. On the fourth year, they would suggest limiting your expenses to show a profit and pay some taxes, even if you didn't a have a real profit. This is a myth. By following the right steps, you will limit your risk of becoming a hobby.

You are selling online with full intent of being profitable. You started your business to someday quit the day job, work from home, work less hours, and make more money. The rules state that all you are required to have is *profit motive*. You just need to prove you have that motive.

Unfortunately, the IRS isn't just going to take your word for it. They expect businesses to act a certain way. If you show the right picture to the IRS, there will be no doubt that you are indeed operating to make a profit, despite five years of bad luck. Some business, not usually retail, are set up to have positive cash flow but will report year after year of tax losses to lower their taxable income due to the differences in tax law and actual cash flow. Some of these businesses have been challenged in court. Because they presented the right picture they won the case and were able to remain businesses preventing the owners from paying thousands of dollars in additional taxes and penalties.

People running online businesses where they are not the primary bread winner for their home really need to pay attention here. This would include small etsy stores, eBay sellers, blogging, YouTube channels, and others. These particular types of small business are great tools for having cash flows but could easily be turned into a hobby if they have several years of losses.

There are five key elements needed to establish that you are indeed trying to operate at a profit and want to grow.

1. **LLC or corporation registered with the state(s) that you are operating in.**

2. **Business bank account that is 100% separate from personal bank accounts.**
3. **Properly kept accounting records that are in accordance with generally accepted accounting principles.**
4. **Written intent to be profitable.**
5. **Functioning as a business would.**

State Registration

A hobbyist is doing something for fun which might make a little money like raising horses that are sold at some point. A hobbyist doesn't think about registering their hobby with the state. A business owner wants some sort of protection in the event of a lawsuit or if something else goes wrong. That protection comes from the LLC or corporation registration.

Business Bank Account

A hobbyist doesn't care if they mix their personal funds with their hobby funds. They are not worried about profit so there is no need to track actual revenue verse expenses. A business needs to turn a profit or it will eventually have to close. A business that is trying to show a profit is going to take the fastest approach to do that by separating personal expenses from business expenses. That way when bank reconciliations are done, there won't be a lot of adjustments.

Accounting Records

Hand in hand with a business bank account are proper accounting records. This unfortunately means tracking all the pennies. This is made a lot easier by having the business bank account. A hobbyist just thinks it's awesome that they got some extra cash and will only be worried about that revenue at tax time. They will thumb through their bank statements and can offset that revenue with plenty of expenses. A business will want to show why there was a profit or loss, analyze it and figure out how to increase revenue in the future. This is done and demonstrated to the IRS by having the proper records.

Written Intent

A hobbyist doesn't care about future goals for their hobby. They are merely enjoying working on the project. A business should have a written business plan, clearly defining goals for growth. If not a formal written business plan at least a set of goals the owners are trying to achieve. Without goals, the business looks more like a hobby as it wonders from day to day just trying to bring in a little revenue.

Functioning as a Business

A hobbyist makes their own decisions and doesn't worry about anything other than their enjoyment from the hobby. A business, especially with multiple owners needs to have board meetings or staff meetings. Keep minutes of these meeting so that the owners can refer to them. Have an annual retreat to discuss the future and set goals. If you are growing and doing more than you can handle, contract out work or hire employees. If you have inventory, do periodic inventory counts and update your records for shortages or obsolete inventory.

Hobbyist don't do these activities. If they have inventory that doesn't sell they will eventual throw it out or donate it to a thrift store. A business owner will keep old inventory for as long as they can to try and sell it to turn a profit.

THE IRS IS STARTING TO INCREASE THEIR AUDITING OF SMALL BUSINESSES, looking for tax revenue by changing the classification from small business to hobby. If you have your ducks in a row, you could be running an actual hobby but still win the argument that it is a for-profit business. Wood shop owners can deduct the purchase of a new table saw because they make something and sell it on eBay later. Another person that sews quilts for fun and sells one or two on etsy can write off the cost of their sewing machine.

Don't lose your standing as a business just because you didn't pay the fee for an LLC registration. The cost in back taxes will be much greater than the registration and annual report fees.

Chapter 4: Employee Benefits – Your Benefits, you're the only employee

For online retail, we want to structure the company as an S-Corp with one fulltime employee, you. All other work that you cannot handle goes to outside help from subcontractors or part time employees. **Why do we do this?** So, we can get 100% of the employee benefits. Yes, we are selfish business owners. But it really is all just a tax strategy.

Most *employee benefits* that can be expensed through a business must follow the rule of *Non-Discrimination*. This means that if you offer benefits to one employee, you must also offer those same benefits to all employees. You can establish a vesting period, and most businesses do, that employees don't receive benefits until they have been with the company for at least one year and are full-time employees. This allows some flexibility if you do have employees, just keep them part time.

There are benefits and drawbacks to both subcontractors and employees. That topic is outside the scope of this book as we are focused on tax planning and savings. For this book, suffice it know that if you do have employees, you should consider structuring your benefit package to exclude them or be willing to give your employees the same benefits that you give yourself. We will discuss this more at the end of the chapter.

Why do we want employee benefits? *The goal is to transition as many personal expenses into businesses expenses as we can.* We do this through employee benefits. Let's consider what the average employee might be paying personally that some large corporations might offer as benefits.

- **Health Insurance**
- **Wellness plans**
- **Medical reimbursement plans**
- **Reimbursement for use of personal items**
- **Retirement benefits**

This is a list of usual benefits; however, some corporation such as Google and SAS offer additional benefits such as catered lunches, scholarship programs for children, massages, and vacation expense reimbursement.

Since we are a small business with one employee I recommend sticking with the usual benefits as you cannot afford an attorney to fight with the IRS.

The IRS has allowed S-Corp officers and owners to discriminate on health insurance, but that is the only benefit allowed to do so. There are multiple steps involved with reporting health insurance expense correctly as it is required to be run through payroll. But this provides an additional benefit because your health insurance is not taxable to Medicare and Social Security while still increasing your wages to reach that 20% amount discussed earlier. By claiming health insurance as a business expense in a S-Corp, payroll taxes go down and so do income taxes. **I always like getting two birds with one stone!**

There are other types of health insurance plans to consider as well. A great option for tax savings and saving on insurance premiums is to get a high deductible health insurance plan, the cheapest one you can find. Then get a *Health Savings Account* (HSA).

The basic concept of how insurance companies make money is by investing in stocks and bonds. They estimate what their payouts are going to be every year and then set their premiums so that they can at least break even on premiums versus payouts. They take these large amounts of premiums and then invest where they can make large profits.

An HSA is the very same idea but for individuals. Insurance companies **HATE** HSAs and thus do not offer them. HSAs are offered through banks. You invest in your HSA like a 401K retirement plan. The Bank then invests your funds in the stock market or bonds. You earn the profits, not the insurance companies. You can withdraw from the HSA to pay any medical expenses. Your high deductible plan covers the large medical costs such as an ICU stay. But you don't have to pay the insurance company profits for all the minor medical expenses. And you can use your HSA to pay the high deductible if something really bad happens.

Just like with health insurance, there are multiple steps to reporting HSA contributions made on an employee's behalf but end the end they are treated as direct business expenses. Unlike health insurance, you cannot discriminate on HSA contributions. But you can set up the HSA program and get the same savings either through your business or individually. There are limits to the amount that can be contributed every year. But usually, the contribution limit is greater than the medical expenses for the year.

Medical reimbursement plans are like HSAs. The difference is that with an HSA you are investing to cover future medical expenses and earning tax free gains. Medical reimbursement plans pay employees for their out of pocket medical expenses. Employees bring in their bills from their doctor and your company reimburses them for the cost. This creates expenses for your company without the employee getting taxable income. But you lose the tax-free investment income in the HSA.

I recommend an HSA over medical reimbursement plans due to the tax-free investment income. However, the reimbursement plan works if you are just starting your HSA and you have medical expenses without enough cash in the account. You can use both together, but if you pay an expense out of the HSA you cannot reimburse that expense through the reimbursement plan as well.

You also cannot discriminate with medical reimbursement plans. Since the point to is to make the expenses business related and if you have full time employees other than yourself, you must provide the same benefits to them. You could restrict the amount on the reimbursement plan such as a dollar limit per year to ensure you are not paying all your cash for a major medical expense for an employee.

Now let's discuss *using personal items for your business* and getting reimbursed for it. Compare this to a regular wage earner working for a large corporation and they are asked to run to the store to pick up a purchase. The corporation usually will have the employee submit a mileage report to reimburse them for the travel expense. Why does the corporation do this? It is because the mileage expense is worth more to them than it is to the employee.

If the employee is not reimbursed, they are able to claim the expense as an *unreimbursed business expense* included in their miscellaneous itemized deductions. Miscellaneous itemized deductions are limited on the individual tax return. In most cases, miscellaneous deductions do not get claimed as they are not over the limit. Then you still must get over the standard deduction before you can itemize. The business can write the mileage expense off at dollar for dollar, no limits applying.

We want to do the same thing with any personal items used for business. The goal is to move as many personal expenses to business as we can. By transferring medical expenses and use of personal items as business expenses out of the itemized deductions to become businesses expenses, then use the standard deduction, we are legally double dipping on the deductions.

The standard deduction was set up to simplify the tax preparation by allowing taxpayers to forgo adding up all the small things that are tax write offs as itemized deductions. But there is not a law against reclassifying the small expenses as business expenses (*within reason*) and still taking the standard deduction. If the standard deduction is exceeded and itemization takes over, do a better job at moving expenses into the business.

So, what are the itemized expenses that you need to pay close attention to?

1. Medical expenses
2. State taxes usually withholding and property tax
3. Home owners' mortgage interest
4. Charitable contributions
5. Miscellaneous
   a. Tax preparation fees

b. Unreimbursed business expenses

c. Investment expenses

Medical expenses we covered above through self-employed health insurance, HSA and medical expense reimbursement plans. Unfortunately, there isn't much we can do with state withholding tax. But property tax we can partially move to the business as well as the home owners' mortgage interest. Property tax, mortgage interest, and unreimbursed businesses expenses we will discuss in the next chapter. Let's first focus on charitable contributions, tax preparation fees, and investment expenses.

There are only two reasons to claim *donations* outside of your business. **1) you are donating to a church or church type organization. 2) Your state offers additional tax credits for donations to certain state ran charities or nonprofits.**

Most donations we want to report as advertising expense through the business. *Why?* We want to double dip. If we can get the standard deduction and still claim donations as an expense we just increased the tax deductions. The argument for this is that we expect to get some form of advertising out of the donation. An example is donating to the construction of a community park where a sign of your business name will be added to the playground. It is hard to make that argument for tithing or cash plate donations at a church.

Some donations might qualify for additional savings at the state level. Some states offer additional tax savings on donations to specific state ran second hand stores such as Goodwill or to state education institutions. You will have to ask your CPA or go to your state Department of Revenue website for additional info. If your state does offer an additional tax credit, it could be more beneficial to report as charitable contributions under itemized deductions and then claim on your state tax return.

(Warning: Soap Box) *Tax preparation fees* should never be reported as an itemized deduction for a business owner. I have seen many CPAs be very conservative and allocate a portion of tax preparation fees to the itemized deductions where it is limited and of no benefit. They do this because they claim that part of the tax return preparation was for items that were not business related. I argue, and a few other CPAs argue, that you only came to a CPA for your business taxes. Otherwise you would have used **TurboTax** or other method to self-prepare. *The tax code was originally written with the intent that any person could prepare their own taxes.* If you are paying for a professional, all the fees to that professional are related to your business. (Okay, I will get off my soap box now.)

Investment expenses result from paying for advice, fees to brokers, or subscriptions to be able to invest in some form or another. Usually the investments are in stocks or bonds through a broker such as Charles Schwab, eTrade, or Wells Fargo Business Advisors. However, you could also have expenses through other forms of investments such as in a friend's business.

These expenses are limited as miscellaneous itemized deduction. It is simple to move all these expenses to your business. Just set up the investments through the business. All large companies invest their extra cash to put it to work for them. You should be doing the same. Do not invest with after tax dollars, invest with pretax dollars by running it as a business account.

If you have a retirement plan, consider setting up a *SIMPLE* or *self-employed IRA* (traditional plans) through your broker to increase your ability to contribute to the plan and take advantage of the tax savings. There are many benefits to these retirement plans. However, I usually recommend using a *Roth IRA* as small business owners.

The difference between a Roth and Traditional is Roth plans are taxed when you put the money in and traditional plans are taxed when you pull the money out. Traditional plans are great for *traditional wage earners* which is what they were designed for. Small business owners are not traditional, *I would argue that they are far from traditional, at least I hope I am.*

The traditional person works all their life receiving a salary. Then when they retire they live on Social Security and their 401K. When that runs out they are a department store greeter. They usually have much less income when they are retired. In this scenario, they benefit from getting a tax break when they were wage earners because they were in a higher tax bracket.

Small business owners tend to retire in higher tax brackets than they were in while running their business. When you are young you have kids at home (*deductions*), you have a mortgage on your home (*deductions*), you have all sort of expenses you can run through your business (*deductions*). Then you hit age 70 or whatever it will be when we can start drawing Social Security, but you don't quit working. **You are self-employed.** If you quit working you will be bored. Even if you sell your business with intentions to retire, your mind doesn't stop working and soon you are starting another business to make money at something else. Not to mention you did *sell* your business and you have an influx of cash.

Your kids have moved out (*hopefully*) and your house is paid off. As I mentioned you haven't really retired so we are still treating your hobbies as a business and writing stuff off. But you are now in a higher tax bracket than you were when you started putting money into the retirement plan, unlike the traditional person. When you started the retirement plan you paid taxes in the 15% bracket, now you are in the 25% bracket. Under a Roth plan, you don't have to pay taxes when you withdrawal from it. You can plan that cruise and pay for it with money that you don't have to pay taxes on. While the traditional person will have to pay their 15% before buying the cruise tickets.

Back in Sunny Day Sports, Frank paid $500 to various nonprofits as neighbor kids came to the house looking for pledges throughout the year. After talking to his CPA, he has learned that his state is like most and doesn't offer additional tax breaks for the contributions he made. He also paid $100 in March for a business version of consumer tax preparation software. He knows he prepared it wrong and feels like he paid too much in tax which is why he went to a CPA this year but we are still going to move that $100 to the business.

Frank is also paying $7,500 a year for health insurance that is added to his wages, bringing down his payroll taxes even more. He had out of pocket medical expenses of $300 and paid $480 for a family gym membership which is included in the company's wellness plan. See column 3 in the Appendix for how these items affect Franks taxes.

Chapter 5: Work from Home and Save on Your Taxes!

There is a great feeling to finally renting or purchasing a physical location for your business. It is a sign of growth and many people have this goal. You can move your stuff in, set up shop and you can finally keep your business life separate from your personal life. Right? **Wrong!** You're a business owner, you will never separate your business life from your personal life. *What have you really done?* **You now have two electric bills, two water bills, two rent or mortgage payments, two property tax payments (if renting, your property tax is included in that rent), you have successfully doubled or tripled all your utility and property expenses.**

If there is a specific reason for a physical location, great, but the business had better be able to pay for it. This would be if you are retail, selling at a local brick and mortar as well as online. CAUTION: brick and mortar retail is dwindling due to online retail.

All eCommerce businesses should be running from home. Again, this is to transfer personal expenses or expenses that could be itemized into business expenses. The only time you should have operations outside of your home is if you are required to store inventory at another location such as Amazon FBA or if your sales volume is just so much that you cannot handle it yourself. Even then I would still try to find a way to store inventory at your home. Consider building an external garage and hiring part time help (*high school kids*) to ship inventory for you. UPS, FedEx, and USPS all pick up at your home no matter the volume.

Two items limit home office deductions. **1) Area where active operations are taking place.** Active operations mean you cannot have any personal items in the same area such as your children's toys or an Xbox. I guess if you are designing video games, or children's toys you could argue both of those, but for the rest of us that is not the case. *Easy fix for this.* If a person shows up at your door saying they are an IRS agent and wants to see your home office, tell them they need to either have a warrant signed by a judge or they need to contact your CPA. **If they insist, call the police, they aren't an IRS agent.** The normal procedure is that you will receive a letter stating that you are under examination and part of that examination includes a review of your home office. This gives plenty of time to get the office in order, for the inspection.

2) Areas where you store business inventory or supplies but you can also store personal items, if it is just for storage. Your garage, if holding inventory just became deductible as well as the shed in the back yard, a spare bedroom, or under the stairs. The more inventory you can stock into any free space the more we can write off as a business expense.

The home office deduction takes the percentage of your home dedicated to office space and multiples it against your utilities, rent/mortgage interest and depreciation, home owners/renters insurance, and property tax to make that portion of your personal expenses business expenses. **We transform nondeductible personal expenses into deductible business expenses.** Unless you absolutely need another location, try to set up your business to work from home. Some of the clients I work with can deduct 50% of their utilities because they store inventory throughout their house.

There are two methods for calculating the home office deduction. The method in the preceding paragraph where a percentage of all home expenses are deducted, is the *actual expenses method* and usually results in a better deduction. But many people have heard this is a red flag for audit. A more commonly used method is the *simplified method* that gives a $5 deduction for every square foot used for business purposes. The simplified method has an upper limit of **$1,500** which is just 300 square feet. I always recommend using the actual expense method as we can easily prove the square footage used for business. As I said before, make sure to clean up the kids' toys before the walk through with the IRS agent. With my clients, I walk through prior to the agent walk through to make suggestions and I walk through with the agent as you should never deal with the agent yourself. I recommend even leaving the house to ensure that the agent cannot ask any questions that should be filtered through the CPA.

Let's return to our example at this point. Frank is running Sunny Day Sports out of a spare bedroom in his basement. This office is 10ft by 15.5ft for 155 square feet. He is also using half of his double car garage for inventory storage, electing to park his car in the driveway instead of the garage which is 24ft by 24ft, making his storage space 12ft by 12ft for an additional 144 square feet. This brings the total business use square feet to 300 (we rounded up for easy math). His home is 2,500 square feet. This gives Frank 12% of all home expenses as business expenses.

When Frank was preparing his return last year, the software asked if he was using any portion of his home for business. He marked yes and put in the square footage. He doesn't even remember if the software gave him the option for the actual expense method but he did what was easiest as the software wasn't very good at explaining what was happening. He got the $1,500 deduction limit.

By switching to actual costs method, Frank can deduct 12% of all his utilities as business expenses. He paid $3,600 for electric, sewer, water, and gas for the year. He rents his home for $1,000 per month and paid $250 for a yearlong policy of renter's insurance. Total expenses for the year are $15,850 times by the 12% equals $1,920 of personal expense that are now moved to the business. That's $420 of additional expenses that he had missed previously. Not much by its self but the little items add up for greater savings.

If Frank owned his home instead of renting he would take 12% of mortgage interest, property taxes, and *deprecation*. Deprecation is the cost of your home divided by 39 years. Then each year take that amount times by the 12%. If the home is $200,000, deprecation on the home each year would be $5,128 times by 12% = $615. The remaining interest and property taxes can still be deducted on the Schedule A, if there are enough expenses to itemize. These expenses are included in column 3 of the Appendix.

Chapter 6: Accounting for Inventory = Headache

Many of the expenses that we have discussed up to this point such as employee benefits are personal expenses that you would have had to pay whether you were a business owner or not, we are just able to change the nature of them into business expenses through various tax laws that have passed, also known as incentives from congress for people to run businesses.

On the other hand, the purchase of your inventory is a direct cost of your business and if you do not keep good records you could end up losing some of those expenses as deduction on your tax return.

Accounting for your inventory properly is one of the hardest bookkeeping tasks but provides one of the largest expenses for saving on taxes. If you lose your receipts and can't remember how much you paid for something you could be leaving expenses off your tax return that you should have taken. This could get expensive fast.

Then if you just guess at how much your inventory costs, you can still lose the tax deduction. *How painful would it be to find out that poor accounting practices resulted in paying higher taxes than you had to because you couldn't prove the purchase of inventory?* It has happened. **IRS agents can deny deductions as the result of not enough substantial evidence to prove the expenses.**

Consider this, many people are purchasing items on sale at department stores and then reselling on eBay or Amazon. If you do not have good inventory tracking methods in place, the IRS agent will just see purchases of goods from that department store such as Wal-Mart. They could easily say those were personal expenses and deny the deduction. Instead of paying taxes on just the net profit from the sale, you now must pay taxes on the revenue. **THAT COULD PUT YOU OUT OF BUSINESS, FAST, AS IT CUTS YOU PROFIT MARGIN DRASTICALLY.**

We want to ensure that every dollar that is spent on the business is listed as a deduction on the tax return and there is absolutely no doubt that they are business deductions. This is the number one reason for a good accounting system. A few hours of bookkeeping or hiring an outside bookkeeper can result in $1000s of savings in taxes.

To better illustrate this point let's return to Frank with Sunny Day Sports. After talking to his new CPA, he then purchased a subscription to Quickbooks Online. He could link his bank account which automated most of his accounting. He decided that inventory was too much for him to handle so he asked the CPA what to do. The CPA offered a reasonable price to have his bookkeeper record sales and deposits from Amazon and record purchases of inventory. Periodically, the bookkeeper sent inventory count sheets to Frank who had to just make sure the inventory count was correct.

This service throughout the year cost him $6,000 at $300 a month. But he could save time by not having to keep track of the inventory himself. The $6,000 is a business expense that is completely deductible. The CPA explained that $6,000 sounds expensive for a small business owner, there is no doubt. But because Frank is in the 25% federal tax bracket and 10% state tax bracket he would save 35% in additional taxes resulting in an actual cost of $3,900. Plus, through this system, Frank and the bookkeeper realized that he had been sending free samples to various customers and bloggers to get reviews on Amazon and blogs. He had forgotten to include those in the past as expenses. They could record an additional $400 in cost of goods sold for the samples sent out. $3,500 was much more reasonable for a small business owner to have the inventory properly accounted. See column 4 in the Appendix.

Chapter 7: Don't Lose a Single Penny

There is a joke that accountants will spend hours looking for a single penny. As a CPA myself, I agree that this is ridiculous. But I have talked to other CPAs that pride themselves on spending an hour looking for 5 cents. They then bill their clients for that hour. I personally like to work in terms of *materiality*, meaning an hour of billable time to find 5 cents is robbery from the client. But, the idea behind the action is still very applicable to all business owners. We don't want to pay a single cent more than we are required to in taxes. That is fair.

The tax code defines expenses as cash outflows that are *ordinary and necessary* to conduct business. There are many court cases and statements issued by the IRS which try to define ordinary and necessary. But with an ever-changing environment, new industries, and more creative accounting methods, ordinary and necessary becomes very murky. Many of the expenses discussed in previous chapters, such as a gym membership for employee benefits could be argued as neither ordinary nor necessary for just about any business, especially e-commerce businesses.

However, many large businesses offer it as an employee benefit and deduct it as a business expense on their tax return. If we are set up as a corporation, then we can use the same arguments they do, and we will let the large companies with deep pockets fight our battles.

A gym membership is ordinary and necessary because if we did not offer it, our employees might leave for better benefits elsewhere. *But you are your only employee.* **Exactly!** If you got paid more and had better benefits why take on the hassle of running your own business? You wouldn't. But you are hoping that after all your sweat, blood, and tears you will make a profit which will be better than you could have gotten as an employee of Amazon.

So, we should offer to ourselves incentives to keep running the company. If we quit running our company to take a job at Amazon, the overall GDP of the country goes down and your local economy suffers because you are no longer bringing in funds from all over the world which you spend (*incentive for the federal government to keep you running a business.*)

The second argument why your gym membership is ordinary and necessary is that healthy employees are better employees. If you use your gym membership to stay fit, you will be more productive than if you don't. **And we want our employees productive.**

In an audit, you just present why the expense is ordinary and necessary. Any sane person will not want to deny a common practice and take the fight to court. That includes the IRS agent.

You will have the backing of some major corporations to ensure that you win. In court, even if the corporation has only one employee who is also the only shareholder, they distinguish between the two. If a precedent is set that a gym membership is no longer tax deductible because it is not ordinary and necessary, there will be a lot of corporations upset that they can no longer deduct that benefit. As a small business, we don't have deep pockets so we do not want to be more aggressive than the big dogs and we can let them fight the battles.

The following is a list of expenses that would likely be considered business expenses. When reading this list, keep in mind the argument above and the terms of *ordinary and necessary*. Ask yourself how would you be able to apply that these expenses are ordinary and necessary for your business. Many of the expenses in this list are often overlooked, even by traditional, brick and mortar businesses. This is also not an exhaustive list. **The idea of this list is to get you to think about what you could be expensing that you are not. We want to make sure you are not leaving anything on the table.**

- Office Furniture
- Cell phone and cell phone bill
- Magazine purchases (related to business)
- Retirement savings
- Rent or mortgage interest
- Property taxes
- Education and training
- Seminars
- Webinars
- Auto expenses
- Utilities
- Travel
- Staff retreat
- Shareholder/owner retreat
- Professional associations
- Travel
- Meals
- Entertainment
- Postage
- Internet

- Website hosting
- Business/liability insurance
- Health insurance
- Employee benefits
- Sales tax you pay on purchases
- Supplies
- Credit card and bank fees (overdraft charges)
- Fuel
- Lawn care
- Advertising
- Charitable donations
- Samples and gifts
- Furniture, equipment, cars, or other items previously purchased and now using in business
- Legal and accounting fees
- Bad debts
- Cleaning services
- Cost of goods sold
- Repairs and maintenance costs
- Family members' wages
- Freight and shipping
- Investment advice
- Newspaper, blogs, economic outlook subscription fees
- Parking and tolls
- Home office deduction
- Membership to small business political groups, lobbies, and clubs.

Remember the goal is to move as many personal expenses to business expenses that you reasonably can.

While attending class at Idaho State University my teacher passed out the 2008 Microsoft Financial Statement filed with the SEC. One of the requirements in the statement is to disclose the amount of aggressive tax stances they had taken. In their report, worded very professionally, was that they had taken $10 million worth of aggressive tax stances that if audited could be overturned by the IRS. Some students thought that was completely incredible and irresponsible that Microsoft would take such aggressive positions. One student asked if the IRS would just go ahead and audit since Microsoft disclosed it. This lead to a long discussion which as I listened, I came to the realization and made the comment that, "Sure they took $10 million in aggressive stances. Even if they do get audited, they will hire some very expensive attorney for $1 million and end up settling outside of court for $5 million." They pay the taxes on the $5 million, about $1.8 million, save $1.8 million on what they got to keep and the $1 million expense for the attorney will result in additional tax savings of $360,000. Had they not taken any of the aggressive positions they would have paid $3.6 million. Instead they are only paying $2.44 million. Microsoft saved $1.16 million in taxes by being aggressive, still getting audited, and hiring an expensive attorney to fight it (*all hypothetical. I don't know if they were audited by the IRS*).

As small business owners, we need to take that same approach to our taxes. **Can you come up with $10,000 of additional expenses that could be considered more aggressive?** Start a savings or investment account to put some of the money away that you save from the additional expenses just in case. Then, if you are audited, present your arguments, and hope for the best. Most audits will go somewhere in the middle as no one wants to go to court, especially the IRS when they are only looking at a couple thousand in revenue. The IRS is the money-making arm of the government.

Ultimately, the IRS must make a profit. If they don't turn a profit, just like any business, they will be replaced.

Also, by being extra aggressive on what we claim as a business expense, we provide low hanging fruit for the auditor to claim as nondeductible. We can consent on those items and fight harder on the more beneficial items. And this is only if you are audited. Chances are that you won't be audited.

So, we settle out of court, something in the middle of the road. You pay the taxes on $5,000 ($1,250), pay $1,500 to the CPA that helped with the audit which results in tax savings of $375. Using the same example just with less zeros, we have saved $125. But that is only if we get audited. We aren't required to disclose our aggressive tax stances to the public like Microsoft is and we are a small fish in a very big ocean. It will probably cost the IRS more than $1,250 to even audit you.

Back in Sunny Day Sports, Frank and his CPA discussed several expenses that Frank had been treating as personal and the CPA suggested moving to the business. These expenses included a used desk that they valued at $400, a webinar for $75, a family vacation turned into a shareholders' retreat for $750, meals where Frank and his wife discussed business for $300 (limited to 50%), and a subscription to a blog with training videos for $15 a month. These total $1,555 in expenses that Frank had been leaving on the table. None of these are overly aggressive that I would imagine getting denied in an audit. These expenses are included in column 4 of the Appendix.

Chapter 8: Supporting your Kids

Did you know that you can turn the money you give to your children into a business expense? **You can!** There are two options to do so.

1) Wages

2) Ownership

<u>START THE KIDS WORKING FOR THE MAN WHILE THEY ARE YOUNG:</u>

There are various laws to protect children from workplace abuse, aka*: child labor laws*. The main one being that you cannot hire a child under 14 years old. Employing your children is a completely different story. You can start working your children at any age. They just should be reasonably compensated for their work. *Reasonable* means that you cannot over compensate them. **If they do a day's worth of work, they can receive a day's worth of wages and their salary can't be comparable to someone with a Ph.D.** And, just like any employee you need to keep good time records of the date and how long they worked.

Similar to the idea of a child earning an allowance for doing chores, now you can turn that allowance into a business expense. They can start small, taking out the garbage, dusting, and vacuuming. Then when they want a toy or a candy bar, it is a business expense, wages. The nice part about employing your minor children is that you **do not owe, nor do they owe, payroll taxes on the amounts they earn. No Medicare, Social Security, or unemployment insurance taxes.**

The one downside is that you will need to file a W-2 for them and they could be required to file an income tax return. The current minimum filing requirement and standard deduction for a dependent is $6,300. This means if they make more than $6,300 of income for the year, they will be required to pay taxes on it. And there is a law, nicked named *kiddie tax*, which requires any taxable income for a minor child to be taxed at the same incremental rate as the parents. This is to prevent people from passing income to their children to take advantage of the child's lower tax brackets. But you can still take advantage of the standard deduction of $6,300.

MAKE THE KIDS THE MAN WHILE THEY ARE YOUNG:

Passing ownership in the family business to your children while they are young can provide long-term benefits. But, you need to understand the potential risks associated with passing ownership.

The main benefit here is like paying wages, only this time they don't have to actively work for you. The idea with this is that you are passing income to take advantage of their standard deduction. This is great for very young children or children that don't live at home. Basically, it is great in any circumstance where the child is unable to actively work for the business.

Because of the kiddie tax rule as discussed above, you can take advantage of the multiple standard deductions by passing the income to your children. Unfortanetly, the IRS has addressed this strategy by limiting the standard deduction on passive income for dependents to $1,050. If their percentage of income from the business is greater than the $1,050, the amount of tax due will still be less than if you hadn't passed the income.

The secondary benefit comes down the road. Everyone is going to retire at some point (*at least we like to dream we will*). Passing ownership in a company to the next generation can be very difficult. To prevent paying tax, the ownership must pass slowly, spread out over many years as a small percentage is passed each year. The more your business is worth, the longer it will take to pass the ownership. By starting your children while they are young, and the business is young or just starting, they can start building equity in the business and you will already be starting to pass ownership.

The downside here is that your child might grow up to be irresponsible or wayward. Once they reach the age of majority (18) your children can have a say in the management of your business. There are various ways around this such as setting up proper corporate articles and bylaws before they turn 18. If all else fails, you are always able to buy out a wayward child. But this is a long discussion and outside the scope of this book.

Ownership is also a way to provide **tax free income** to your children down the road. As they build equity in the company, you can then issue them dividends to pay for college, help to purchase their first home or various other items. They are getting a return on their investment on which the taxes have already been paid.

Whether you pay them wages and/or give them some ownership in the business, you could start them an investment or savings account for some of their wages/profits, which they can draw on later. Then when they come to you to ask for some cash to buy a new toy, get that candy bar, or need a new dress for prom, they can buy it using the money they have earned, just like you do, money that was tax free by utilizing their standard deduction.

CAUTION DANGER:

We hear stories in the news about kid stars growing up and suing their parents and always wonder what happened. Usually, it is because the parents spent the money they child earned. If you make your child an employee or owner and pay them dividends or wages you are required, by law, to provide that money to them. You are the trustee over those funds while they are under the age of 18. You can provide those monies to them in the form of birthday presents or candy bar from the store. But, once they turn 18, you are no longer the trustee of those funds.

Frank, when first discussing his situation with his CPA, decides to pass a small ownership to the children. Frank also likes the idea of putting the kids to work to help with the family business. He has them clean the office and take out the trash every day. As they get older he is going to let them help with shipping and other tasks. Frank ensures that between their ownership percentage and the wages they are making, each child earns at least $6,300 to take advantage of their standard deduction. Any amount the children earn over that does not matter in the analysis of tax savings since that income is taxed at Frank's tax rate and he will be paying it anyway. This is presented in column 5 of the appendix.

Chapter 9: Conclusion

Prior to going to the CPA, Frank owned $28,698 in taxes with an effective tax rate of 28.7%. By changing to an S Corporation, paying himself a salary, paying his kids a salary, starting the employee benefits, and taking the actual expenses for his home office he cut his taxes by $20,272. He saved over 70% of the original amount that would have been due. Based on the actual cash flow from Frank's original taxes on the Schedule C, he is only paying 8.43% in taxes. **That is less than the lowest tax bracket of 10%.**

That is better than a person making $100,000 in salary at Amazon who is paying around 20% in total taxes. Frank is still carrying a lot more risk by running his own business but now he is getting compensated for that risk, which makes the anxiety worth it. Instead of just working to pay taxes to the government he is seeing a return on his investment of blood, sweat, tears, and money.

Preparing taxes using these strategies should be done with professional help. Unfortunately, even many professionals fail to advise their clients of these strategies. This is partially because many CPAs today are hesitant to work with clients that are running online businesses. The older generation of CPAs don't understand the eCommerce niche and fail to apply the tax savings strategies that are available to all business owners.

If you are working with a CPA already and they haven't mentioned these types of ideas to save on taxes, you need to consider changing CPAs. You are paying that person to help you save on taxes. If you are leaving money on the table because of poor advice, don't pay them. You are better off preparing your taxes on your own and savings the preparation fees. Seek out a CPA that understands your industry and is willing to work with you instead of just taking what you give them and putting it straight into tax software. Year after year of saving $20,000 in taxes adds up. If you run your business for 30 years, that is $600,000 in actual cash savings. Even if your CPA charges you $10,000 (*which I think is way too high*) you are still coming out ahead.

Appendix: Sunny Day Sports Taxes

Sunny Day Sports
Tax Planning Taxes Due

	Reported Schedule C	S-Corp Election	Employee Benefits	Additional Expenses	Paying Kids
Chapter	N/A	Ch. 2	Ch. 4-5	Ch. 6-7	Ch. 8
Total Sales	200,000	200,000	200,000	200,000	200,000
Costs of Sales					
Costs of Good Sold	75,000	75,000	75,000	75,400	75,400
Freight	10,000	10,000	10,000	10,000	10,000
Total Cost of Sales	85,000	85,000	85,000	85,400	85,400
Gross Profit	115,000	115,000	115,000	114,600	114,600
Operating Expenses					
Internet	1,000	1,000	1,000	1,000	1,000
Advertising	300	300	300	300	300
Camera	2,000	2,000	2,000	2,000	2,000
Shipping Supplies	500	500	500	500	500
Auto Expense (Mileage)	2,700	2,700	2,700	2,700	2,700
Merchant Fees	5,000	5,000	5,000	5,000	5,000
Bank Fees	2,000	2,000	2,000	2,000	2,000
Total Operating Expenses	13,500	13,500	13,500	13,500	13,500
Tax Planning Expenses					
Dad's Wages		20,000	11,500	9,500	7,500
Kid's Wages					12,600
Wellness Plan				780	780
Health Insurance			7,500	7,500	7,500
HSA			5,000	5,000	5,000
Home office Reimbursement		1,500	1,902	1,902	1,902
Additional Expenses			600	8155	8,155
Total Tax Stratagies Expenses	-	21,500	26,502	32,837	43,437
Net income	101,500	80,000	74,998	68,263	57,663
Home Office Deduction	(1,500)	-	-	-	-
Schedule C Taxable Income	100,000	80,000	74,998	68,263	57,663
Other Income		20,000	11,500	9,500	7,500
Total Income	100,000	100,000	86,498	77,763	65,163
Deductions					
Deducitble part of SE Tax	(7,497)	(1,530)	(880)	(727)	(574)
Less Standard Deduction	(12,700)	(12,700)	(12,700)	(12,700)	(12,700)
Less Personal Exemptions	(16,200)	(16,200)	(16,200)	(16,200)	(16,200)
Total Deductions	(36,397)	(30,430)	(29,780)	(29,627)	(29,474)
Taxable Income	63,603	69,570	56,718	48,136	35,689

	Reported Schedule C	S-Corp Election	Employee Benefits	Additional Expenses	Paying Kids
Chapter	N/A	Ch. 2	Ch. 4-5	Ch. 6-7	Ch. 8
Taxable Income	63,603	69,570	56,718	48,136	35,689
Income Tax					
Federal Income Tax	8,616	9,509	7,581	6,291	4,424
State Income Tax	5,088	5,566	4,537	3,851	2,855
Total Income Tax	13,704	15,075	12,118	10,142	7,279
Self-Employeed Income	98,000	20,000	11,500	9,500	7,500
Self-Employeed Tax	14,994	3,060	1,760	1,454	1,148
Total Tax Due	28,698	18,135	13,878	11,595	8,427
Percentage of Income	28.70%	22.67%	18.50%	16.99%	14.61%
Total Savings		10,564	14,820	17,103	20,272
Tax Due/Original Tax Due		36.81%	51.64%	59.60%	70.64%
Tax/Original Income		18.13%	13.88%	11.60%	8.43%

CPSIA information can be obtained
at www.ICGtesting.com
Printed in the USA
LVHW07n1734030918
589015LV00007B/68/P